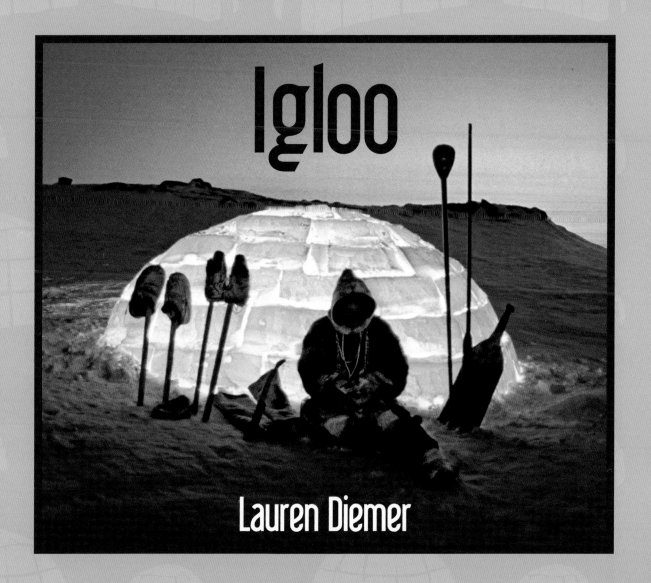

Igloo

Lauren Diemer

Weigl

Published by Weigl Educational Publishers Limited
6325 10th Street SE
Calgary, Alberta T2H 2Z9
Website: www.weigl.com

Library and Archives Canada Cataloguing in Publication

Diemer, Lauren
          Igloos : Canadian icons / Lauren Diemer.
Also available in electronic format.
ISBN 978-1-77071-585-1 (pbk.).--ISBN 978-1-77071-578-3 (bound)
          1. Igloos--Juvenile literature. 2. Inuit--Dwellings--Juvenile literature.
I. Title.

E99.E7D53 2010   j971.9004'9712   C2010-903750-2

Printed in the United States of America in North Mankato, Minnesota
1 2 3 4 5 6 7 8 9 0 14 13 12 11 10

072010
WEP230610

Editor: Heather Kissock
Design: Terry Paulhus

Weigl acknowledges Getty Images as its primary image supplier for this title.

Every reasonable effort has been made to trace ownership and to obtain permission to reprint copyright material.
The publishers would be pleased to have any errors or omissions brought to their attention so that they may be
corrected in subsequent printings.

We acknowledge the financial support of the Government of Canada through the Canada Book Fund for our
publishing activities.

CONTENTS

What is an Igloo?

What sort of house do you live in? Is it made of wood or bricks? Imagine living in a house made of snow and ice. This is an igloo.

Canada's Far North is known for its cold winters. In the past, the **Inuit** of northern Canada would build igloos for their winter homes. Igloos helped keep the Inuit warm by blocking out the wind. Some people still build these snowhouses to keep warm.

5

Who are the Inuit?

The Inuit are one of Canada's Aboriginal Peoples. Almost half of Canada's Inuit live in Nunavut. The rest live in northern Quebec, Labrador, and the Northwest Territories. Most Inuit live in small towns and villages. Some can be found in very **remote** parts of Canada's North.

Why Build an Igloo?

In the past, the Inuit were mainly hunters. They followed animal herds as they **migrated** with the seasons. The Inuit needed houses that were easy to build. A house made of snow met these needs. It could be built within two hours. An igloo was left behind when it was time to move.

Today, some Inuit still build igloos to live in while hunting. Igloos are also built as shelters when the Inuit are travelling.

9

Big and Small

Igloos can be large or small. Some igloos are big enough to house 20 people. These igloos are made up of small igloos that are joined by tunnels. Other igloos have only one large room. One family lives in these igloos. The smallest kind of igloo is big enough for only one person. These igloos are built by people travelling on their own.

Building Blocks

Igloos are made from blocks of snow. To make a block, the snow must be packed together. The snow must be hard so that it can be cut out of the ground without falling apart.

Blocks are cut out of the snow using a saw or knife. Large blocks are cut for the bottom of the igloo. Small blocks are cut for the top.

Dome Sweet Dome

Igloos are shaped like domes. To make the dome, each layer of snow blocks must be placed on a slant. A circle is made on the ground with the first layer of blocks. This circle sets the size of the igloo. Layers of blocks are then placed on top of each other to form the igloo's walls and roof. The top block is the last one to be placed.

Igloo Extras

Over time, people have added special features to igloos. Some people place a block of ice in the wall of their igloo. This acts as a window and lets in light. A short tunnel can be built at the entrance. The tunnel serves as a doorway. It also helps to keep out cold winds. Sometimes, the walls on the inside of the igloo are melted by a flame. The melted walls are left to freeze again. The ice layer adds strength to the walls of the igloo.

Inside an Igloo

The Inuit often cover the floor of their igloo with animal furs. The furs provide warmth. A stone lamp is placed in the centre of the igloo. The lamp is for light and warmth. Some people even put a stove in their igloo. To cook inside, the igloo must be **ventilated**. This allows the smoke from cooking to escape.

Heat rises, so the sleeping area is on a platform that is higher than the entrance. Here, warm air from body heat, lamps, or the stove is trapped.

Toonik Tyme

In spring, Iqaluit, Nunavut's capital city, holds a festival called Toonik Tyme. The festival celebrates Inuit **culture**. There are events based on Inuit **traditions**.

One event is an igloo building contest. People race to build an igloo in the fastest time. Then, they must stand on top of the igloo to prove that it is strong. The person who builds the strongest igloo in the shortest time wins the contest.

Build Your Own Igloo

Supplies

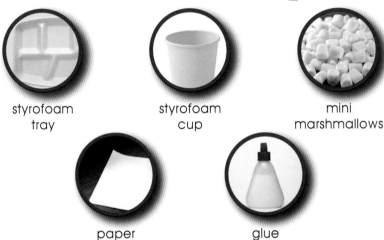

styrofoam
tray

styrofoam
cup

mini
marshmallows

paper

glue

1. With an adult's help, cut 2.5 centimetres off the top half of the cup.

2. Turn the cup upside down, and glue it to the styrofoam tray.

3. Glue a row of marshmallows around the base of the styrofoam cup.

4. Continue to glue more rows of marshmallows around the cup until it is covered

5. Stack a few marshmallows to one side of the cup to make the door to the igloo.

6. Your igloo is now complete!

Find Out More

To find out more about igloos and the Inuit,
visit these websites.

How to Build an Igloo
www.nfb.ca/film/How_
to_Build_an_Igloo

Arctic Voice—The Inuit
www.arcticvoice.org/
inuit.html

Toonik Tyme
www.tooniktyme.com

How Igloos Work
http://people.howstuffworks.com/
igloo.htm

Glossary

culture: the ideas and activities of a group of people

Inuit: one of Canada's Aboriginal Peoples

migrated: moved from place to place

remote: far away from other towns and people

traditions: information, beliefs, or customs that are handed down through generations

ventilated: allowing air to come into and leave a building

Index